Visit and Learn
Gettysburg

by Martha Hubbard

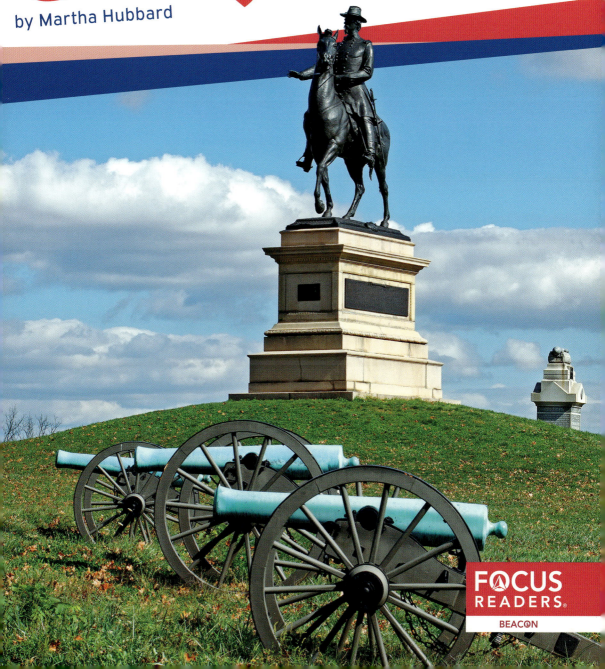

FOCUS READERS.
BEACON

www.focusreaders.com

Copyright © 2024 by Focus Readers®, Lake Elmo, MN 55042. All rights reserved. No part of this book may be reproduced or utilized in any form or by any means without written permission from the publisher.

Focus Readers is distributed by North Star Editions:
sales@northstareditions.com | 888-417-0195

Produced for Focus Readers by Red Line Editorial.

Photographs ©: Shutterstock Images, cover, 1, 4, 7, 10, 12, 14, 19, 22, 29; Historical Views/agefotostock/Alamy, 8; iStockphoto, 17, 27; Tim Brown/Alamy, 20–21; US National Park Service, 25

Library of Congress Cataloging-in-Publication Data
Names: Hubbard, Martha, author.
Title: Gettysburg / by Martha Hubbard.
Description: Lake Elmo, MN : Focus Readers, [2024] | Series: Visit and learn | Includes bibliographical references and index. | Audience: Grades 2-3
Identifiers: LCCN 2023008712 (print) | LCCN 2023008713 (ebook) | ISBN 9781637396179 (hardcover) | ISBN 9781637396742 (paperback) | ISBN 9781637397848 (ebook pdf) | ISBN 9781637397312 (hosted ebook)
Subjects: LCSH: Gettysburg, Battle of, Gettysburg, Pa., 1863--Juvenile literature. | Gettysburg (Pa.)--History--Juvenile literature.
Classification: LCC E475.53 .H836 2024 (print) | LCC E475.53 (ebook) | DDC 973.7/349--dc23/eng/20230308
LC record available at https://lccn.loc.gov/2023008712
LC ebook record available at https://lccn.loc.gov/2023008713

Printed in the United States of America
Mankato, MN
082023

About the Author

Martha Hubbard is an Ohio-based author with a background in teaching and school librarianship. She enjoys learning and sharing what she has learned through her books. When she is not reading or writing, Martha loves taking long walks outdoors and spending time with her family and three dogs.

Table of Contents

CHAPTER 1
Honoring the Dead 5

CHAPTER 2
The Battle of Gettysburg 9

CHAPTER 3
Turning Point 15

A Faithful Friend 20

CHAPTER 4
Visiting Gettysburg 23

Focus on Gettysburg • 28
Glossary • 30
To Learn More • 31
Index • 32

Chapter 1

Honoring the Dead

The wind blows across empty fields. **Statues** glow in the sunshine. Old cannons rest in the grass. People walk quietly through a **cemetery**. They are there to honor the dead.

 More than 600 cannons were used in the Battle of Gettysburg.

5

Gettysburg is a national military park. It is where the Battle of Gettysburg was fought. This battle took place during the US Civil War (1861–1865). The battlefields are filled with **monuments**. Fallen soldiers lie in the Gettysburg National Cemetery.

At least five women fought in the Battle of Gettysburg. They disguised themselves as men.

 A statue of Brigadier General John Buford stands in a battlefield.

Today, many people visit Gettysburg. They tour **historic** buildings. They walk through the battlefields. They learn about an important event in US history.

Chapter 2

The Battle of Gettysburg

The Civil War **divided** the United States. In the North, many people opposed slavery. But in the South, most white people supported it. In 1861, a group of Southern states tried to break away from the Union.

White slaveholders forced Black people to do backbreaking work.

 More than 160,000 soldiers fought in the Battle of Gettysburg.

Their leaders wanted to start a new country. That set off a war.

One battle took place near the town of Gettysburg, Pennsylvania. It happened in July 1863. The battle lasted for three days. It was very bloody. The North won the battle. But both sides lost many soldiers. Approximately 50,000 people were killed or hurt.

US leaders wanted to honor the soldiers who died at Gettysburg. They chose land for a cemetery.

One **civilian** died during the battle. She was standing in a kitchen. A bullet came through a door and hit her.

 Lincoln's Gettysburg Address lasted for only two minutes.

In November, people gathered for a **ceremony**.

President Abraham Lincoln traveled to Gettysburg. He gave a speech. He talked about the fallen soldiers. Lincoln's speech was short. But it became famous. It is known as the Gettysburg Address.

Lincoln's words reminded people what they were fighting for. Lincoln said he wanted to keep the Union together. He also wanted all people to be free and equal.

Visitors can tour the David Wills House in Gettysburg. That is where Lincoln wrote his speech.

Chapter 3

Turning Point

Gettysburg was a turning point of the Civil War. Before the battle, the South's army had seemed strong. So, the South's leaders tried to **invade** the North. They planned to attack Pennsylvania.

Robert E. Lee led the South's main army. Lee was a slaveholder.

They hoped this would make the North give up and stop fighting.

However, the plan did not work. The South lost the Battle of Gettysburg. After that, its army was much weaker. Now it had no chance of ending the war quickly.

Two years later, the South lost the war. The Union stayed together. Slavery came to an end.

Today, many visitors travel to Gettysburg. They learn about the battle. They see where it

 Robert E. Lee (seated, left) surrendered on April 9, 1865.

happened. Visitors can walk on the battlefields. These fields are filled with many monuments. There are more than 1,300 in all.

17

Some of the monuments are for Northern states. Some are for Southern states. Other monuments are for military **units**. And some are for individual soldiers.

Visitors can also see living history **demonstrations**. Every July, people reenact the battle. Actors wear

Gettysburg has one of the world's largest collections of outdoor sculptures.

 A monument for a military unit (left) stands near the Pennsylvania State Memorial.

uniforms. They pretend to fight. They fire cannons and guns. There are loud explosions. Smoke fills the air. This event gives visitors an idea of what the battle was like.

THAT'S AMAZING!

A Faithful Friend

An army unit from Pennsylvania had a dog. Her name was Sallie. She joined the unit as a small puppy. Sallie saw many battles. At Gettysburg, she got separated from her unit. But a few days later, her men went back and found her. She had stayed with some soldiers who were hurt.

Just before the war ended, Sallie died in battle. Her men buried her on the battlefield. A statue of Sallie is at Gettysburg. It lies at the bottom of the unit's monument.

Sallie is one of two dogs that have statues at Gettysburg.

Chapter 4

Visiting Gettysburg

Most visitors begin at the museum and visitor center. The museum teaches visitors about the Civil War. Weapons, uniforms, letters, and other objects are on display. There are also movies to watch.

A statue of Abraham Lincoln sits outside the museum and visitor center.

Other parts of the museum let visitors hear stories from soldiers who fought in the battle. This information helps visitors understand what they will see on the battlefields.

The visitor center has a huge painting of the battle. The artwork circles a large room. The painting is 377 feet (115 m) around and stands 42 feet (13 m) high. It took more than a year to paint. The room also has sound effects and flashing

 The large painting in the visitor center is known as the Gettysburg Cyclorama.

lights. Visitors feel like they are in the battle.

On the battlefields, tour guides discuss the history of each place.

They help visitors understand how the battle unfolded. And they tell stories about the people it involved.

Visitors go to the cemetery as well. Remembrance Day takes place on November 19. That was the day of the Gettysburg Address. Each year, there is a parade. People also put candles on the graves. They

Did You Know?

Since 1934, more than 130 million people have visited Gettysburg.

 People put flags on soldiers' graves for Remembrance Day.

read the names of the soldiers who died. These actions help people remember the battle's importance.

27

FOCUS ON
Gettysburg

Write your answers on a separate piece of paper.

1. Write a paragraph describing the main ideas of Chapter 2.
2. If you visited Gettysburg, what would you be most interested to see? Why?
3. Where can visitors find a large painting of the Battle of Gettysburg?
    - **A.** the museum
    - **B.** the visitor center
    - **C.** the cemetery
4. Why did the South invade Pennsylvania?
    - **A.** If the North lost land, its leaders might think the war was not worth fighting.
    - **B.** If the South won a battle in Pennsylvania, it could easily take over all of the North.
    - **C.** If the two sides fought in Pennsylvania, they would stop fighting in other states.

5. What does **separated** mean in this book?

*At Gettysburg, she got **separated** from her unit. But a few days later, her men went back and found her.*

    A. kept close
    B. moved together
    C. left alone

6. What does **reenact** mean in this book?

*Every July, people **reenact** the battle. Actors wear uniforms. They pretend to fight.*

    A. to fight for real
    B. to act out a past event
    C. to do something dangerous

Answer key on page 32.

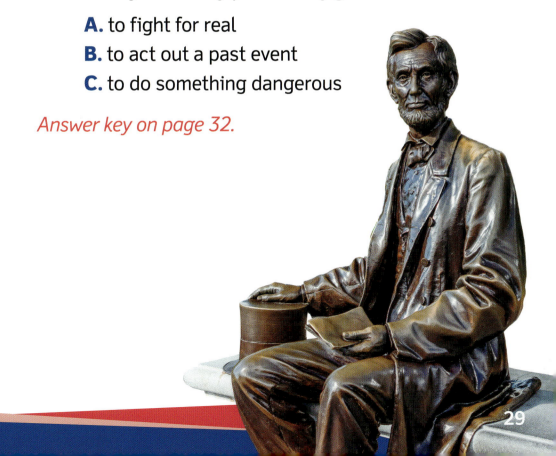

Glossary

cemetery
A place where dead people are buried.

ceremony
An event that honors a person or celebrates an important event.

civilian
A person who is not in the military.

demonstrations
Events that teach people how something works or how something was done in the past.

divided
Caused something to come apart.

historic
Important in history.

invade
To enter in large numbers in order to conquer or take over.

monuments
Buildings or structures that are of historical interest or importance.

statues
Pieces of three-dimensional art, often showing people.

units
Small groups that are part of a military.

To Learn More

BOOKS

Gale, Ryan. *Fact and Fiction of the Civil War*. Minneapolis: Abdo Publishing, 2022.

Smith, Elliott. *Slavery and the Civil War: Rooted in Racism*. Minneapolis: Lerner Publications, 2022.

Yomtov, Nel. *Abraham Lincoln and the Gettysburg Address: Separating Fact from Fiction*. North Mankato, MN: Capstone Press, 2021.

NOTE TO EDUCATORS

Visit **www.focusreaders.com** to find lesson plans, activities, links, and other resources related to this title.

Index

B
battlefields, 6–7, 17, 20, 24–25

C
cannons, 5, 19
cemetery, 5–6, 11, 26

D
demonstrations, 18–19

G
Gettysburg Address, 12–13, 26

L
Lincoln, Abraham, 12–13

M
monuments, 6, 17–18, 20
museum, 23–24

P
painting, 24

R
Remembrance Day, 26–27

S
slavery, 9, 16

T
tour guides, 25–26

V
visitor center, 23–24

Answer Key: 1. Answers will vary; 2. Answers will vary; 3. B; 4. A; 5. C; 6. B